SKIPSTONE

Ginny MacKenzie

The Backwaters Press

Winner of the 2002 Backwaters Prize in Poetry

All poems Copyright © 2003 by Ginny MacKenzie

The author wishes to thank the School of Visual Arts and David Rhodes for all the support over the years (and Maryhelen Hendricks and Bob Milgrom of the English Department for their patience and smiles)—and all the kindhearted folks at BMCC—CUNY, the Ragdale Foundation and the Virginia Center for the Arts. And a special thanks to poets Donald Justice, Bill Knott, and Louis Phillips, for their encouragement and editing comments.

And, of course, for his dedication to producing this book, thanks to Greg Kosmicki.

Backwaters Press logo designed by L. L. Mannlein
Copyright © 1997 by The Backwaters Press

Cover photo by John Berthot © 2003

All rights reserved. No part of this book may be reproduced in any form, except for the inclusion of brief quotations in a review, without permission in writing from the author or publisher.

First Printing, 800 copies, June, 2003

Published by: The Backwaters Press
                Greg Kosmicki, Editor/Publisher
                3502 North 52nd Street
                Omaha, Nebraska 68104-3506
                (402) 451-4052
                gkosm62735@aol.com
                www.thebackwaterspress.homestead.com

ISBN: 0-9726187-1-6

Printed in The United States of America by
Morris Publishing   3212 E. Hwy 30   Kearney, Nebraska   68847

Acknowledgments:

The author thanks the following journals and anthologies where these poems first appeared, sometimes in earlier versions:

Agni Review: "There, Where the Grass Breaks"
Artful Dodge: "Academic Dreamlife"
Boulevard: "Going Out"
Koroné: "Mother, Your Last Word"
The Literary Review: "The Immortality Coffee Shop"
The Little Magazine: "At Home," and "Provence Weekend"
The Madison Review: "Street Smart"
      reprinted in *The Random House Book of Verse*
Mississippi Review: "An Invitation"
Mudfish: "Sneak Around"
The Nation: "Getting Through"
North Dakota Quarterly: "The Coming," and "In the North, My Father Faces Death"
Pequod: "He Paints a Picture of His House, " and "Cezanne's Father"
Ploughshares: "Aunt Lena Committed to Bellefonte State Hospital," "Mary Magdalene at the House of Simon the Pharisee," "Retreat to the Country of Pure Drought," and "Skipstone"
Poems & Plays: "The Artist's Child's Birthday Party"
The Seattle Review: "Clearfield County Fair"
Seneca Review: "On the Cellar Floor, A Shadow"
Shenandoah: "Lucia Drawn as Santa Zita by Francesca Alexander for *The Roadside Songs of Tuscany*, 1883"
Slant: "The History of Sound," and "Women in Kunai"
Threepenny Review: "Tintoretto to His Apprentice"
      reprinted in the *Anthology of Magazine Verse and Yearbook of American Poetry*
Whetstone: "The First Married Painters"
Whiskey Island: "There"

from The Judge's Statement

SKIPSTONE is a book both smart and passionate, filled with poems whose words pump color back into language while they both frame and release our best and worst memories. At once traditional and iconoclastic these poems urge their readers to accept the human mysteries of love and art—"don't look/beyond the window to where the grass breaks like a fever/above the entrance to Hell." For Persephone and her mother both, for all mythological and other lovers, delight anneals—as this fine poetry does.

Hilda Raz
2002 Judge

For my son, John,
                    my bright light

And to the memory of my aunt, Ardythe Beish Bailey

SKIPSTONE

I

CLEARFIELD COUNTY FAIR	1
AUNT LENA COMMITTED TO BELLEFONTE STATE HOSPITAL	3
SNEAK AROUND	5
THE CHESTERFIELD PEKINESE	7
FOR THE CHEERLEADERS	8
WHIPLASH	9
AT HOME	10
FATS	11
THE WEST BRANCH	13
RETREAT TO THE COUNTRY OF PURE DROUGHT	14

II

THERE	17
STREET SMART	18
AN INVITATION	19
THE ARTIST'S CHILD'S BIRTHDAY PARTY	20
HE PAINTS A PICTURE OF HIS HOUSE	22
WHEN THE DOG WAKES UP	25
THE FIRST MARRIED PAINTERS	27
NOTES FROM A MAINE VACATION	29
GOING OUT	33
THE SCIENCE OF MIRACLES	34
MILKSHAKE OPUS	36
THE IMMORTALITY COFFEE SHOP	37
A POET'S LIFE	38
MY GIRLFRIEND DATES A WORLD-RENOWNED SEX THERAPIST	40

III

THE MUGGING	43
MOTHER, YOUR LAST WORD	45
THE COMING	47
IN THE NORTH, MY FATHER FACES DEATH	49
DRIVING MY DAD	51
ON THE CELLAR FLOOR, A SHADOW	52
GETTING THROUGH	53
THE ADVICE	54

IV

TINTORETTO TO HIS APPRENTICE	57
CEZANNE'S FATHER	58
BATTLEFIELDS	59
PROVENCE WEEKEND	61
TESTIMONY	63
MARY MAGDALENE AT THE HOUSE OF SIMON THE PHARISEE	64
WOMEN IN KUNAI	65
LUCIA DRAWN AS SANTA ZITA BY FRANCESCA ALEXANDER FOR *THE ROADSIDE SONGS OF TUSCANY,* 1883	66
THE HISTORY OF SOUND	67

V

SKIPSTONE	71
TRESPASSES	73
SMALL FACTS	74
ACADEMIC DREAMLIFE	76
THERE, WHERE THE GRASS BREAKS	78

SKIPSTONE

Ginny MacKenzie

I

CLEARFIELD COUNTY FAIR

My mother told me never mind the *morphodite*—
"And stay away from those babies,
in those bottles," she called out the screendoor.

Their abortive faces bulged their jars:
some lacked noses, or ears; others
had double sets of genitals—labeled

For Educational Purposes Only, they
were lined up like targets. I stepped back,
took imaginary aim. Just that morning

I had scattered starlings from our garden
with my BB gun. Shooting galleries, kewpie
prizes, Haunted House—I passed them all.

Lit by a red spotlight: Mondu the Hermaphrodite
loomed, glowering at us as if we
were to blame for the half-rouged, half-bearded

cheeks, —for all this. I closed my eyes,
thought of that other display, what they'd've
been like grown up. Then suddenly

it was over, or nearly: "Ladies,"
the barker hissed, "I must ask you to leave.
Gentlemen, for another 50 cents,

2 quarters, 5 thin dimes, Mondu will remove
this loincloth and reveal to you…"
Back outside, it was chilly, the fairgrounds

covered with trash. I headed up the midway toward home, my new Babydoll high-heels sticking in gum, taffy, Crackerjacks.

AUNT LENA COMMITTED TO BELLEFONTE STATE HOSPITAL

Because he'd heard menopause was hard he forgave her
the unmade beds, the cold meals—
what he couldn't accept was the way she looked:
the slip all yanked down below her dress,
the hair pasted with grease and sweat
to her neck like wet crepepaper.
The hospital would have to come and take her.
In those days, in those small-towns, what else
could you do with a wife like this—a good wife
and mother falling into the things around her.
No matter what, it does matter what people say
and their breath filled with accusations...

That was all thirty years ago now. I don't
know any more of the story, they're all dead
or gone away, or why it matters to me,
why I lie awake nights sometimes thinking about it,
imagining Lena still alive somehow,
though delirious, senile by now. I see her there.
I visit her there: I sit across from her
and watch her scrawling a crayon over
some scratch paper, which she asks me
to slip out the window as if there were
someone down there, waiting for a message.
Sometimes I try to read them. Here
and there I make out what seem to be words:
blouse or *searchlight*...

Sometimes in the morning I wake up
from a dream of her and start to worry the things
in my house are like hers were back then,
when her bad time came—a sinkful of dishes,
the laundry-hamper spilled down the stairs...

Or I'll hear someone at the door:
only the deliveryboy probably, wanting his money,
saving up to go to college. There's just
no future, he says, in these small-towns.
There's a place for everything but you
can't find it in its place. He's out the door
before I can say yes, yes, I agree.

SNEAK AROUND

At the playground a pinafored
girl pushes a boy on his swing

up into uncluttered air… In rare
sibling agreement, my brother and I

sat at the top of green carpeted
stairs we'd quietly bump down,

one step at a time—symbiotic
shadows—slipping on hands and

knees into a livingroom of aunts,
and uncles, an occasional Sunday-night

cousin. Then we'd sneak around.
Under an aunt's chair, we'd tie

the strings of her scuffed
oxfords to the chairlegs; she

went right on talking. Ready
to leave, she'd say, "How did

this happen? Tied like a log to a
raft." I would shush my brother,

whose eyes were lost in shadow from
the lamp with the orangish shade

that kept the room a timeless color,
kept us tying grownups to their

seats as gangsters. Ardie, our
favorite aunt, tolerated us longest

in the cave under her chair, then
died too young of a hushed illness.

THE CHESTERFIELD PEKINESE

Uncle Bill swore snub-nosed Chester
and his stubby brother, Field, —
two Pekinese—could say "I love you."

"Now Chester," Bill would ask, "How
do you feel about me?" and Chester—
though it could have been Field—

would put his flat nose up against
the air, his neck bending till
it looked orgasmic, and moan,

"ee woove wooo." "I love you too,"
Uncle Bill would say, repositioning
Chester under his left arm to balance

Field's position under his right—
next to his heart. Then my uncle
would drop to the sofa and say,

"A virtual Shakespeare, no?" When
we begged him to let Chester—
and Field—do it again, he'd say

they were no longer in the mood,
and he'd return to his greenhouse
to repot succulents and sing

"The Yellow Rose of Texas" to his prize-
winning roses—in iambic pentameter,
if you counted right, Uncle Bill said.

FOR THE CHEERLEADERS

A flag in each hand, cowboy hat pulled
2 gallons down over my hair, on my shoulder
a white braided cord. Kick, kick
the red skirt past my hips, circles
of wow at my waist. Light the batons,
the ends becoming black coconuts.
Oh they're thrilled. They love me,
my red circle, my cunt, my patriotism.

WHIPLASH

My parents are Mr. & Mrs. Monty Hall
3:30 to 4 every afternoon,
giving away my aunt's inheritance,
her house. The newlyweds who won it
have graveled the lawn, excised
the umbrella trees from the backyard.
I spent whole summers with my aunt
under those trees.
She died in winter.

Downstairs, humming, my mother
vacuuming without her glasses on,
sucks the crumpled skin of a snake
into the hose—but it's a broken necklace
that rattles until she stops and fishes for it.
She fumes—of course, I'm at fault,
though I'm upstairs in traction,
my head floating
from the pull of a water bag
hooked to the closet door.

AT HOME

The TV is still on, as my mother drifts to sleep
on the couch. Upstairs, my father's dream shifts;

a fear of thunderstorms he's been able to keep
from his wife all these years...The frontdoor cracks

up the middle. She wakes so hard, so fast she thinks
he's dead; he sleeps so soundly she can only wait,

afraid what this heap of splinters, this cannonball
at the foot of the door, could still do:

The laughter of vandals rings down the street.
This will cost a lot—the explanations, the repairs.

The late news is over and his thunderstorm heads
farther north—ice breaks up on the river and he's

caught there, wringing his hands...Later,
the cannonball looks hollow, though it takes both

of them to carry it down to the cellar. They wonder
if you could crack it open and put your hands inside.

My father would like to sell it but is afraid they'll
have to keep it, —in the cellar, safer out of mind.

FATS

Martha's dog Minnie Mouse's
hair is so long it dusts
the floor. She looks
like a cross between
a ragmop and a wind-up
doll. "Wouldn't you think
that hair down there
would wear off?" Martha jokes
for the nth time—this time
rousing her bored son
who stomps out slamming the door,
scaring poor Minnie into the pantry.
Martha pauses, seems thrown
offstride more at losing half
her audience than
her son's rudeness, then
plunges on with us: "Remember
Denny McDougal? Remember!
Always picking fights—he
spent more time picking himself
off the floor than he spent
on the barstool. Hey, Gene,"
she nudges my father and points
at me, "you ever tell your
daughter about the night you
shot pool with Minnesota Fats?"

I start to smile before she
even begins, I know what's coming.
"Remember what that Fats said
when he stepped up to the bar?
'When I drink, everybody
drinks...and everybody pays!' "
she belts out the punchline,

and we all laugh on cue…
I wonder if I'll be laughing
with friends like this when
I'm seventy, repeating the same
exaggerations, half-remembrance,
half-truths, articles of faith—
the old stories to ward off old age.

I remember Mother once telling
me something about Minnie, how
she had to be rescued from
the man in the nextdoor trailer.
She still shies from men,
it seems. I start to ask Martha
what happened, what he did
to her, then decide not to.
Aside from Minnie, the stories
are what they like best,
stories they've probably never
even begun to forget: like
Denny throwing a punch
at Fats after he beat Dad.

THE WEST BRANCH

They will canoe the Susquehanna
from beginning to end. At night, she dreams
of underwater births, the canyons
downstream. Her father dreams of currents,
an exit at Curwensville Dam.
He lived near there once, had a trillium patch
and spoke with a Scottish brogue.

In shallow water they hit a rock, are stuck
on a ledge. They paddle-dance out.
What she sees determines his strokes.
At the dam, people travel in motorboats.
The man doesn't judge them.
His daughter does.

The West Branch of the Susquehanna
is classic: clear, just fast enough,
the best weather, the best story
of a man and his daughter. If I could,
I would add a red fox on the bank.
They drift by without paddling.

RETREAT TO THE COUNTRY OF PURE DROUGHT

In every direction drought breaks this land down
to the lapses, the scraps of itself: water
recoiling from the riverbank like sin, sparse crops corroding
in the fields where a crow's
tailfeathers scratch up the ground's faintest color—
drooping, the trees split...

I feel as highstrung as a woodharp, its
sweet sharp whine, —here
I can banjo me miles of wheat
dying, streets vacant of small farm-town dusk, shades
drawn against the heat, thin bickering husbands,
thinner wives—here
I can kick the parched leaves and grin imagining
plowshares tearing the cracked topsoil for nothing, all
the plows plowing emptier and emptier circles—until a
dust devil plucks them up for her hairdo—tornado!

From the bridge
I survey the water level lowering without alarm,
it's enough for me those cattails
down there: sleek-eared survivors of every condition,
every given—they look like torches snuffed out in blood.

If I picked one
and used it as a brush
to paint my self-portrait—wouldn't
it mire, smear me in the shapes
of this dead place, this land it rules? ignoring
my desires for another, better-attended riverbank?

II

THERE

Everyone says I should be thinner, it's
not enough to just take off the baby's
weight, I should diet, starve myself.

In my mouth, a wobbly strand of spaghetti,
a straw stuck deep in a chocolate
shake. Life gets sweeter nearer the end,

I plan to eat more, you won't find a coffin
big enough. After the birth, something's
still unborn, something about baby-sitting

my Great-Grandma, stony elephant legs, us
on the swing, her unable to remember anyone's
name—all those names those mothers

consumed so no matter what might go wrong,
that baby's name wouldn't. Heaven is a
womb. I should know. "Baby boy, I love

you." I gurgle to my newborn, thinking about
the long years ahead of us, my huge body
all the wherewithal I need to stay there.

STREET SMART

At a year old my son saw, really saw,
for the first time, a streetlight. Moon,
he said, happy to see on his corner
the white globe from picture books—
brighter even than he'd imagined.
I was sorry he thought a pedestrian
object like that the moon.

I took it seriously. I'd failed
to provide him an understanding
of a major poetic symbol, capable,
as it was, of changing size and shape and color—
large red harvest moons, cold thin slices
of winter moons. The moon controlled the tides...

Moon, he said pointing at that sad
city streetlight and clapped his hands
like a wind-up toy. Now, years later,
when I travel, I look out my motel
window and see dry leaves blowing
in spirals across the highway
and headlights, little moons—

AN INVITATION

You're not mistaken. You are invited to dinner.
Come talk with my husband, the painter.
Come visit my son, who will listen.
Do not loiter.
Send word you arrive as a poet.
Bring your wife, who is not.
Do not stop to ponder my reasons.
Decide now.
I'll roast goose till its juice turns yellow.
We'll drink wine from the Rhine River border.
Relax with the music I choose for you.
Tell your wife I have the fondue she likes.
Come formal.
A black tie would be nice for the goose.
A red dress would work well for the paintings.
I hope you like endives.
My husband will fix them. He cooks better than I.
I have green liqueur for later.
Perhaps your wife will try it.
If not, I will serve my favorite.
It's sweet but goes well with dessert.
After the music, we can walk to the river.
Rain is not due until later,
On Sunday.

THE ARTIST'S CHILD'S BIRTHDAY PARTY

It is almost night. The cake is gone,
clown plates cleaned, songs done.

A simple card game is going on.
The child, in his still-neat blue suit

smiles. There are few children present.
Mostly, his father's friends stay

to talk about painting. In hushed
tones, late into the night, they discuss

cadmium red, lead white, El Greco's
light, —occasionally the child's

disposition. They say he seemed
subdued, muted almost, not at all

like Picasso's *Blue Boy*. None
of the artists have children.

They prefer to uncle this child.
They hear the mother speak about

the time children take. They don't
want to stare beyond their studios,

to listen at a child's door—far
into the night. But they applaud

the child's drawings. It is before
art lessons—and years—will

persuade him to make likenesses.
This is the time of propeller planes

whose crooked bombs fall upward
and explode into flowers, whose

pilots wear capes like Superman
which hang from their chins and flap

out to their ears like clouds, or
rainbows. It will be a long time

before the child competes with them,
before he knows the difference between

Chagall and Watteau. His young father,
who will mature into the best artist,

will lose his purity of heart…
His marriage will fail. But now

it is late and he leans over to tell
his son to take off, for bed, his blue suit.

HE PAINTS A PICTURE OF HIS HOUSE

1.

This morning he thinks he sees
his house clearly: reds, whites
ochres streaked and flawed as a face
without eyes. His wife
is tired already, her papers
stained by breakfast, the coffee
sours her stomach. The children
are as usual in trouble—
the pantry walls have been covered
with space-monsters murdering
each other with ray-guns.
Crayons roll on the floor.

He comes to the end of the backyard,
enters his whitewashed studio;
it's time to paint, to start with nothing…

2.

Should he paint the house as it was
new, before he moved his family in—
or before any family moved in?
He sees that first family arriving
in their horse-and-carriage, the blues
of that bright morning and all
it promises. They ride near, drawn
into focus. Should he tell the reason
they're here, why they've been brought
to this house they lived in, in another
time, or should he leave some things
to their imagination?

His composition will convince everyone
that this is the way the house was
back then: the muted, somber tones
of that first, perfect family—
their walled-in expression, their posture.
Maybe the sky should be stormier.

3.

This imaginary picture is already better
than trying to capture what he thought
he saw from the corner of his eye:
his wife pocketing a letter addressed
to him, the dollar bill he was sure
was a ten until he got no change: with
a gesture that seems no more than a mere
flick of the fingers, a line appears,
a blue background establishing values.
A bit of green brings forward a rectangle
—not a doorway but one of his children.

4.

Emerging from the underpainting
is a light area he can't identify
or remember painting but which will wake him
later that night as a window pane rattling or
a creaky hinge, and he'll shiver as he opens
the bedcovers and puts on his workclothes.
His wife turns over, stretching out into
his side of the bed—she's still asleep.
On his way to the studio he adjusts
the children's covers, loops a sweater
around his neck.

5.

He squeezes half a tube of red
on that spot of light it seems he
always leaves, always returns to
out of dreams so sound his wife
is sometimes afraid for him.
In spite of the bright studio
lights, the yellow looks muddy,
sunk into itself.   The green's dull.
Even the blue is no longer
that first morning's blue, it
has soared, high above the chimney,
a night blue, a blue that overpowers the family.

6.

He's still there, bent over that blue.
Outside his studio the wind grays
the morning landscape into the black-
and-white of a dream: a slow, old-fashioned
horse-and-carriage moves up the road
and stops to ask directions of a man;
they seem a bit surprised by his manner,
his paint-stained clothes. He stands silent
looking up at them, wondering if all this—
the family and their bright carriage,
the terribly lazy day—if these things
really belong here, in this scene. Then
in a gesture of trust and recognition
he decides it doesn't matter. If their presence
is not incorporate with the white,
the reds and the golds, he'll paint them out.

WHEN THE DOG WAKES UP

> *Never before had anything looked so blank,*
> *My life, these words, the paper, the gray Sunday.*
>
> —Donald Justice, *Variations*

If I had a sister, I could say it was she
who tore through my room like a runaway
train, sending my papers into corners
where words grow dusty. Or perhaps the weather—

the thunder and lightning—split me from my dreams.
I could blame fear, age, insomnia… I can't invent a sleepy
town symbolic of the one I've been away from.
Calvino did it better. And the Renaissance. If

it hadn't happened, I couldn't have spent time
at the museum: Rembrandt's portraits tired my eyes.
And the dragonfly I grabbed at and caught?
The iridescence fluttered on my fingertips for hours.

I felt a flutter of memories, fireflies I chased as a child,
those small flashing bodies I believed plugged
into the ground. Maybe it was that piano sonata
on the radio. It was lovely. It made me think of Sassetta,

the dragon's thighs quivering under St. George's sword.
Or the sound of night snow falling, night flowers
growing. When morning flaps open my eyes,
my dog, warm and rested, opens his eyes. I hear

my mother's voice, or husband's, or son's
and imagine their shapes rustling down the hall
into the deep recesses of the kitchen—
flooding the house with possibility.

THE FIRST MARRIED PAINTERS

She picks up a stick and
lays down red for the antelope's
wary eye, outlines two
hooves into legs skinny
as kindling twigs.

He will fill in black
when his half
of the drawing dries,
though he doesn't remember
if it was white or black
he'd do the tail in. At mid-back,

they meet—husband and wife—
just as they'd planned.
He admires her red,
says the drawing is
perfect—like their life

together. They don't know
about writing—documents
that will separate future
husbands and wives from
one another, assign the art
to one, or the other.

One day he decides to paint
in a neighboring cave.
She visits, surprises him
at work—this time another woman
holds the red. A wrenching

of oh's leaves her throat,
an exiting of their
life she's kept protected
inside her. Stick in hand,
she starts on the old wall:
nothing about meals,

or a shared bed and children,
nothing about a future at all.
Instead, she erases her half
of the antelope and draws
a frame around his, locking it in.

NOTES FROM A MAINE VACATION

(For my son)

The lake stretches wider than my arms,
at night narrowing into a kind of quarantine
that stifles the walls, dulls the windows
till I can no longer remember whether
friends who call me were or were not
once lovers. I must get up soon, change
the lightbulbs, to a lower wattage. Children
always leave and there is no way
of stopping them. Nights pile up

like dark clouds, like menacing dreams—
in last night's you were a bird trapped in
an elevator shaft, I was on the roof
trying to reach you but my arm
was too short. Each morning I wake up
composing the same inane invitation:
arise, roost with me, make these fears
specific...You want to know if I'd be
a mother again? Well, imagine a bird
camouflaging her eggs. It's a challenge.

***

Maine people are practical,
already chopping wood in August for the hard
winter and many have lived alone so long
they're slow to speak—so gone into
the meaning of what they'll say,
they don't bother to find words.

Today I found my way to a clearing. I was excited
to be able to see that far and to be warm,

but then I thought: it's just a meadow. Still,
I did reach the other side of these woods,
a place I imagined to be
a long way off, and I stood there, in that arena
of light for a long time—just looking back.

* * *

Once, in the middle of the night, when
I was very young, I heard
thrashing about downstairs: chairs overturned,
the couch, curtains tangled and pulled
onto the floor…My mother said, "Don't worry,
it's only your father. A bat got in
from the alley…" But I never saw him
that angry, wracking the broom back
and forth over his shoulder, breaking it
finally, on the back of a chair.
I think it was the only chance he ever got
to fight like that for his family.

* * *

Cartoon animals in a magazine: opulent ducks
in silk top hats, fish in chairs, ballooning
dresses. Everything bulges. The lake's distorted
by waves from a passing wind, more
distractions, the same trickery. Everyone's hurrying
to leave. The loons are preparing to migrate
which means they must learn to fly again.
Each year they come north, anchor on this lake
and forget how. In early August they begin
their lessons—a few feet higher each day.
Already by the 11th month, the textbooks
say, infants can recognize their house. Since
there's nothing that memory doesn't change,
at what age do they stop recognizing it?

* * *

Recently I've become quieter, exhausted,
weak somehow—it's like being caught robbing
a woodpecker's nest, the brood inside my blouse
fluttering against my stomach. I know my intentions
are good—but I don't know what they are.
So when I write you, at night, in this notebook
it seems as if I should share some wisdom
but instead write of the day's end, how
sometimes I think I know a little of it,
since as slow as night falls, the days race
through my head like cold downpours dousing
what insights I may have had—I think
if I knew how to swim I'd try
this lake, risk swallowing mouthfuls
of woodlice. This morning, a flock of butterflies
covered the fir trees and meadow
shrubs like orange swampleaves catching the sun
on their wings. They are content, it seems,
with such things, their foraging focuses them.

This is the wettest August since 1971, the third
coldest since record-keeping. I've begun
to float in these facts, these dispensations.

* * *

The Maine sky is really clear, big. You must know
when we look at a star we don't see it
as it is now but as it was centuries ago,
and, if it happened to be destroyed soon after—well,
we see it anyhow. It's like being on the edge
of something, a cliff, and looking down,
and thinking of falling—or it's like
old photographs, daguerreotypes,

that show people nobody knows, rows and rows of them
seated, or standing, all for the same caption: me.

* * *

Constant dreams you're drafted
and your father and I go with you
to an auditorium. Other parents are there.
A play on stage—in the first act the recruits
are shy, understated, but by the second act
they're accomplished comedians ("before" and
"after" what?) I weep—the guns are right there,
safe on their hips. The world's end could begin
as an audience like this watches its sons
prepare for it: a roar over rightstage.

* * *

I apologize for this mother thing—
this looking away from myself toward you
like vacationers at a map. Summer here
in Maine should be easier,
but I find the whole year returning.
It defines me. I often use the survival
technique young mothers must learn:
how to catch sleep wherever they can,
whenever, in any light. The days
drag by, slow as my unending entry
into your absence…

GOING OUT

The mouse stuck between
the ceiling and upstairs' floor darts
back and forth over my head
like an insomniac houseguest—

I get dressed up and consider
excuses for a trip
to town or anywhere I could return from
with a few anecdotes, a new

dancestep. The lake
is so still even the orchids
look like they're swimming. It's
quiet but downtown,

in the village, it could be
quieter: a rock
about to fall. Thud, a dog whimpers.
I go to the door to see but see

myself in the hall mirror. I can't go
to town like this.
Not alone like this. And yet
it is morning, choices exist,

the streets unlocked from their names.
The phone rings: you ask
me to come be with you. I'm frightened
by my own body, how fast it moves.

THE SCIENCE OF MIRACLES

So the clerk could make a proper
fit, my right then left foot
was slipped into the ominous gray
machine, absorbed the assault,
the shock. I got the loafers

or Buster Brown's and skipped
to school, one, two, button my shoe—
a safe life. None of us thought
Superman vision could stop
us, kill us like the husband

of a composer I recently met
who'd had cancer in the old days
when they used unfocused X-rays.
Now, all that radiation
was coming back, like time bombs,

like childhood memories.
He'd already lost his bladder.
She played the new sonata
she was working on as she talked—
D major or F minor,

I can't remember which.
I imagined the untouched organs
of her husband's body,
the lucky parts, waiting
to be held, as if in a vise

or by a careless lover. She said
each time he goes to the hospital
he takes his favorite stones.
He's a rock-hound, a collector.
We live surrounded by superstitions.

Today, I saw a shoeless woman addressing air.
It sounded to me as if she was saying,
two-two, four-times-two, equals me.
I liked her rambling attempts to find
a solution to something somewhere

that must be bothering her.
Like equations, I wish I knew
if those foot X-rays were forming
a battalion, a sneak attack, —if we'll
all die of ordinary precautions.

MILKSHAKE OPUS

> *What do we live for if not to make
> the world less difficult for each other?*
>
> —George Eliot

The only sound now
is a churning icy
chocolate shake in chic
Tribeca—the only sound
here, anywhere. Oh,
this is peace—spitting
hisses of creamy curlicues
penetrating the inner
ear, mild vertigo.
Moonlight cuts
through an arc of
the *Cosmos* window,
lands on my hat.

And though I leave
sweet chocolate
foaming like sentiment,
the waiter points
to the writer's booth,
beckons, as if
to himself, but being
modest, he desires
only to go home.
"Ad infinitum,"
I tell him, pulling down
my hat. Winter
waits on the east side.
"Ad infinitum."

THE IMMORTALITY COFFEE SHOP

If I see neighborhood
women, their hoary heads
nodding, "We are old, we
stick together," it means
another oracle is right.
They are guaranteed
their wisdom. I decide

I'm old. Really old.
I spread my shopping bags
on two chairs, immune
to the waiter's stare.
I say I own this one—
the Immortality Coffee Shop.
I advertise: "Eat here
and you never eat anywhere

else." Jam, muffins,
a vase shaped, amazingly,
like a sphinx. Did I say sphinx?
Maybe, outsmarted by someone
mildly Oedipal, it leapt
from the table creating
a thousand ceramic

gravestones. The busboy sweeps
it up while the waiter
seats sainted mothers, —as if
mothers could be devils—
here, where the dead
already spill their secrets.

A POET'S LIFE

My postal clerk has a *thing*
for me. He says
he's never stamped
a poet's mail before.
He also has the worst
case of chapped lips
I've ever seen. Looking
in a mirror he's positioned
on his desk, he controls
the line so he gets
at his window only women

with promise. He puts
lip balm on when I approach,
rubs his thumb over red
Priority stickers so gently
I ask him not to stop.
"I like your pigtails,"
he says. *"Ponytails,"* I say,
"there's a difference,"
and agree to meet him
for a French film.

Of course I don't go.
The next day one of
my freshmen writes:
*this teacher has hair like
a shaggy dog's* on my evaluation.
I excuse him—he doesn't
know I'm a poet.
My creative writing
students *know* I'm famous.
They've begun wearing
long skirts, white hose,

ponytails. I accuse them
of plagiarizing a poet.
They deny they copy me.
When a friend calls
and says she's playing
a poet off-Broadway
and wants to wear pigtails—
ponytails, I say—
but won't if it upsets me,
I say it's O.K.
I go. She does. I'm upset.

After months of sending me
to other windows, my
postal clerk takes me
back at his window.
He felt jilted but has—
at last—forgiven me.
He asks me to go to
the Fabergé display.
I agree but don't show.
Only in America can a poet
be this successful.

MY GIRLFRIEND DATES A
WORLD-RENOWNED SEX THERAPIST

I would run, dear friend, if a sex-therapist
asked me out. Better, you say,
a New York shrink than an Italian
businessman. In Florence,
men at candlelight trysts
talk into mobile phones—penile extensions
they can't leave alone. Do men,
you ask, make love, always
to themselves, their object of desire?

To some, I answer, sex is a release,
as if "coming" in an egg cup would do the job
as well. Ask your shrink about that.
Now, you say, he complains
your stomach's fat, you're only pretty
sometimes. Dear Janet, I would run. Hide.
Let him have his million dollar bills,
stored beneath his bed, flat,
forever young. He can, in need,
reach down there—pull them out.

III

THE MUGGING

I wait for the blood leaking
between my brain and skull to drain—
afraid if I move a finger or disturb
the perfect-tucked hospital sheets,

my sight will leave me as it did
when the mugger threw me into
the sidewalk. I awoke blind,
saw only dead-white. I thought

I was back in my third-grade
science class, a movie on molecules
about to be projected onto a blank
screen. Would Eddie dare to throw

spitballs at me? Then, a paramedic
was giving me facts. This blindness:
the optic nerve's defense to a shock
it couldn't adjust to. Childlike

I was powerless over the insult
of attack. Would density and shape
and color return? He said so…
Oh, Mother, I know you visit me

and I want to take you into
that night but my breath pulls me
back. I look out the window,
my wishes degenerating

on the sill, but when I look away
from out there, you disappear.
Laid out, arrayed on a monitor-lit
pillow whose starched white

enfolds my head like the hood
of your favorite coat, the one
you seem to wear, still,
in all my dreams of childhood.

Only then they had iron lungs
and oxygen tents. I worry
the bleed is worsening, spreading
downward, entering my body—

paralysis, I expect, is next.
The pain robs me of continuity.
Whole days pass, or minutes.
After the concussion comes prayer.

I must relearn how to slip
my feet over the side of the bed,
to thrust my weight, to take
a first step, hoping I do not collide

with the child in my dreams
who counts hopscotch—sprawled
across the sidewalk, sacrificial,
her hands reaching up to enclose yours.

MOTHER, YOUR LAST WORD

It must have been your last word
like a grape on your tongue
lolled a dark dance through your mouth.
Astonished, you must have swallowed it

or spit it into the air
where it bruised the empty house.
Purple as birth or wet sassafras.
Could it fill me up now with you

the way water filled up
your lungs? A round syllable
forming a name. God? Dad
obeyed you, kept your illness

secret. In the yard he sprayed
aphids from the ferns,
listened at the door. The day you died,
though, was so normal. A Thursday.

Like most things you did,
you did this alone, no one saw
how your heart hurt you, brought
you down like a vine unwinding.

You looked thin on the coffin's
puffy cushioning. People thought
you'd lost weight. I corrected them.
I said it was the embalming—

You taught me truth:
your hair wasn't that red,
you weren't thin.
I call *Mother*. But names,

you would say, are convention
not the substance of our bloodline,
not the dark folds of the throat
that hide the lies we live by.

THE COMING

I

I never made it home to Scotland
so before I die I'd like you to go,
my father told me and like a good

daughter I move through this land,
through fog, uncertain of what
it is he wants me to do. Lightning

over the moors, and beyond, the sea
pounds out its thunder. Tonight
a distant churchbell yields up

a confusing song, a heavenly port
from all this nature. I am unable
to distinguish fact from fairy tale—

until I know something of its history,
this land won't reveal its secrets.
Yesterday a calf lay dead in the road

and a raven swooped down to feed
and I thought, if there were a man
with hair black as that raven, skin

fair as noon, with cheeks red
as calf's blood, I would love him.
But alone, I spend my time

ordering my thoughts, so barren this far
north. I imagine I see three small
birds bring one drop of honey between them

only to leave with three drops of blood.
The road cuts straight through
a brace of hills. There's not a sound

as I stand before an ancient cellar
opening. It seems music comes floating
up out of darkness, a sirensong—like

bagpipes stuck in position to sharpen
certain notes. It tempts me. It's said
that those who were *fairy-glamored*

in the old days were lured down
into these cellars to be seen no longer—
no longer *fairy-glamored*, I walk away.

II

It's as easy to feel at home here
as it is to count to ten. More
than a bloodline, I imagine a life here.

The future sometimes leads to the past
and Scotland stretches out into the north,
hanging out over the Earth as if

it were weightless. I mouth, "Lochs,
Lochs." A sixteenth century churchyard
is filled with my dead ancestors—

their demise foreseen by the Brahan Seer.
The raven drinks three fulls of my clan.
On the Isle of Black, I set legends down.

IN THE NORTH, MY FATHER FACES DEATH

Look at me. It's you you see.
You are the father. So am I.
Outside, snow crackles,
and your smile tightens like a skull.
Your body won't quit.
You want it to. You want to be
where the dead go. You don't want
to see your children grow old.

Your heart almost stops at night,
you say. The nurse instructs you:
"Blow air out from your lungs
like you blow out candles on a cake."
But you're terrified you'll live
to see another December birthday.
If I asked you how you've come

this far, I know, if you could,
you would say, "My father's single
act of love: wrapping me
in his fur-collared coat."
A cold wind awakens you
from your starched pillow, scaring
your spirit, which glances at me.

I will grieve your image,
my first map of the world.
I wish, like some ancient mapmaker,
I could restore order,
but you live inside yourself now.
You must hold yourself in your arms.
In my front room, in my own house,

someone breathes—more real to me
than you. It is your birthday
and deep into winter, when light
is indifferent. I study
skeletal trees through a worn blanket.
No letters arrive from you,
but then they never did. This winter
could kill me, it's so sad.

DRIVING MY DAD

After your death, I try
to understand how
you guarded so well
your silence.
When I'd ask to talk,
to do something with just you,
you'd never answer.
I still think no one hears me.
Sometimes I feel I've found
a piece of your life: your love
of the end of summer, those
cool nights on the backporch.
Tell me you love me for driving you.
Tell me you never learned to drive
so you could ask someone
for something. And sweetheart,
it did keep you home—none of us
would ever see you driving away.

ON THE CELLAR FLOOR, A SHADOW

I am always catching sounds that code
and decode while the dishwasher is on or

the dryer going. My brother is always
shooting the same deer over and over. Skinned,

it swings wildly, in the cellar, an iridescent
color. I inhale the flavor of apples,

clean my slippers of mud from porchsteps
where it drags, its muscles leaking.

Its mouth, doughy, hangs open, drips
snow. I can't always tell by listening

what is happening in the woods: shimmering
branches, shaking clouds, a code.

We give each other conviction. Faith
comes more slowly. I want to pluck the deer's

vertebrae—they are so clear, like strings
on some ancient Chinese instrument. Why

look back? Why make connections? My brother,
you are still shooting that same deer.

The wind blows homeward. We feed it
when we make noises greater than ourselves.

GETTING THROUGH

Worms are turning darker.
The soil creaks like a sleek
new suitcase. Farmers seal up

their windows—I walk away
from everything, head back
toward the clearing where once

my brother settled, silencing
the ground. Everything's
as quiet as when someone closes

his eyes and chants, or
rather counts, to a hundred,
at the start of a hide-and-seek.

THE ADVICE

I dreamed in my sleep again
and again I searched for the door.
You said come to bed, it may appear
by morning.

    Here are bowls of cereal, cream,
azaleas straining at the window.
My sore shoulder reminds me
of last night's debate. I finish
my coffee, leave the house,
prop open the door
behind me.

    I look back at the house:
through the window you are pointing out to me
the animals, flowers, a changing wind.
I agree, things are perfect.

IV

TINTORETTO TO HIS APPRENTICE

Titian? That old hypocrite? You know
he was my teacher once, always lecturing me
on the virtues of earth colors—but I knew
what he meant. Finally he kicked me out
of the workshop; that dock is where
I went to ditch those touched-up sketches
he made me do. I stood there gloating
till they all sank. If those fat-head merchants
could see my smart ships, my Adriatic, they'd
forget his doges, his pious redeemers. Do you
see those masts as bare lines? and lower—
that yellow bird turning everything
below it blue. Good lad! Remember the light
in Milan: my Venice will emerge golder than that.
When my paintings are shown, Titian will see
that I paint his landscape as pure color.
By now, he must be pondering purple; to him
the mountains must seem like wreaths
and mourning robes. One of the framers
visited his studio yesterday, and there,
on his worktable, stood a giant candelabra.
And what was stuck in its stem-holders,
instead of candles, I mean?
nine brushes, stiff with black paint.

CEZANNE'S FATHER

*(To Louis-Auguste Cezanne while sitting
for the portrait "The Artist's Father," 1866)*

It must be hard to pose—you,
a banker and hurried committeeman.
Is the new accountant getting
the clauses of that deed-of-sale right?
You are tired of your son's
obsession. For some reason,

on his fifth birthday, you gave him
a small box of colors. He painted everything;
bridges covered the walls of your home.
When your father exclaimed, "C'est le pont
de Mirabeau," you felt a twinge of
betrayal. Years later, after Paul was hit

by a child on a street corner in Aix,
he could not bear physical contact,
anyone's touch. Calluses thicken
on your elbows, you think of moving
your arms. You are always the subject
of anxious brushstrokes.

The finished portrait will hang
in the National Gallery, the sun
shining directly on your hat,
turning your hair whiter.
Beside the painting, Paul's words:
"Je peint des petits sensations."

BATTLEFIELDS

Not only is she washed
clean, makeup off, a peach
of a girl, and not only
does she lie, sweetly,

beneath the green eyes
of her father, but she
must not quiver, her heart
not quicken when he's over

her. "Someone you don't
know," he says, "saw us
walking and thought you
my wife…" To please him,

arm-in-arm, she goes
with him, anywhere. And when
the Roxy's heavy drapes
spread open, sucking in

strands of her hair, she's
glued to *All Quiet On
the Western Front*. Chests
split apart: one dead

soldier, she decides, a dead
ringer for her father,
whose foot is stuck
snugly in the crack

of his chair. Rocking
in hers, she imagines
herself with a bayonet.
"I'd stick it in all

of them," she thinks
—but not only does
her father smile, pass
her candy, kill her

with kisses, but also the turret
gunner destroys a tank
of Germans, his trigger finger
greasy from popcorn.

No one wins. Drapes
drag shut, she spits hair
from her mouth. If only
old age would sneak

up her father's pantlegs
like an infantryman,
leaving him for dead;
her, a life to lead.

PROVENCE WEEKEND

It was midnight when I arrived at Provence Mansion.
The invitation of Paul Girault promised a grand weekend
and it might have been if I hadn't seen the nude body
slumped in a puddle of blood on the black leather chair.
It didn't take a genius to spot the lifeless stare on her face
and hear the horses pounding the ground behind the stable.

It was Gertrude Hollingsworth from the school by the stable,
my old English teacher, with a copy of *Famous French Mansions*
in her lap. I could taste the sweat rolling down my face.
There was no escaping. It would be a long weekend.
I pulled down a curtain and threw it over the chair.
Even alone, it seemed right to cover the body.

It was then I saw the crumpled note lying beside the body,
a suicide note addressed to a man who worked in the stable.
It puzzled me that a woman planning suicide could sit in a chair
and coolly write, "After having spoken with Paul from the mansion
this morning, I do what I must do this weekend.
I am too old for him. There are wrinkles on my face.

In this cruel light, you can see how age has ruined my face."
I hated Girault, imagining how he must have rejected her body
and I knew it was an old story unraveling here this weekend.
How, in her frustration, Gertrude searched for love in the stable
and disappointed again, asked Girault to invite me to the mansion.
Then, embarrassed, ended her life in this cold leather chair.

All that's left now is to close her book and move the chair
from the window. The porchlight shining in on her peaceful face
proves her point. I wonder if Chan would close the mansion.
I marvel at how the head can hate the body!
My own paunchy stomach reminding me I'm no young stable
boy. God, to think I could have gone yachting this weekend.

Five minutes in this place has seemed like a whole weekend
and already I know it's no suicide victim in that chair.
I have phoned Inspector Cluny. He can question the stable
hands and insist that Paul Girault kiss Gertrude's face.
It was murder. The clue was in the note by the body.
The police can take over. I will be leaving Provence Mansion.

Oh yes: Gertrude Hollingsworth only stopped to admire a mansion.
She would never have used a redundant phrase in the body
of anything she wrote: bad grammar made her wrinkle her face.

TESTIMONY

> *(In 1250, Julia of Belrose was
> found guilty of infidelity with
> Geoffrey of Fontainebleau and
> sentenced to burn at the stake.)*

A fire of oak wood. I want to run
through it, my dress untouched
by the flames. Would that prove my love,
to expose myself to you and hold you
with charred hands? Look at your hands,

my lover. If you choose to, write it down:
my melting sash, the red on my ankles.
It's not just for you I say this.
Your eyes remain calm; mine water
from smoke. The air is so hot, a bird

drops in flight. The crowd, believing it
a sign, cheers the burns on my legs,
lunges in to thrash at my backbone.
Then you are offering me water, I think:
or I see it in your eyes.

I would have deceived you too. I should have
become a witch for real, creating
heaps of branches that are solid trees,
a nun, a whore. You end it here:
your eyes on me, memorizing, revising.

MARY MAGDALENE AT THE HOUSE OF SIMON THE PHARISEE

Simon's house was elegant,
with spacious apartments.
I like to think lilacs
fell from my hair.
Simon himself was dignified, secure.
It was a supper of powerful men;
I crouched under the table, at the feet
of the man I loved, applying ointment
to His feet, out of the usual desire.

Tonight the table is set again,
the same gold plates, prisms
in the goblets. Simon's cleaned
his feet, convinced I am about
to pick the new Savior.
I like to think I won't crawl
under the table. Simon smiles.

Outside the house a girl is begging,
as a man approaches from a crowd of others,
eyes on her bare shoulders, keys
jangling from his pocket. She watches me
through the window, holds a bowl.
His eyes are fixed. My legs are numb.

WOMEN IN KUNAI

Men in our village dream of a pig-run
in the ginger, burn the slopes
to find it. I have my mother's skill
for spotting birds and coaxing them in
from the bay.

A roast pig for my birthday!
My mother enters the kunai grass, animal tracks
already under her feet. She releases
the arrow but the men dash
from the ginger and plunge their spears
into her throat, hide her body in the roots—
a woman in the sacred hunting grounds.

That night I steal out past the huts,
the grasses scraping my skin. Moonlight,
at last I find her body sprawled
in a ditch, put it into a string-sack,
sweet potatoes over her head.

In a secret place away from the village
I cover the body with coconut fronds
and every day go to consult it.
Larger and larger fish stream from her nostrils
until one day nothing but water and foam.

I invent a canoe, an outrigger,
a large ship with tall masts.
Then an airplane, threshing machine
and canned goods. All these
I secure in the kunai with ropes
of sweet spiced hair, where no one
will ever find them.

LUCIA DRAWN AS SANTA ZITA
BY FRANCESCA ALEXANDER
FOR *THE ROADSIDE SONGS OF TUSCANY*, 1883

On the path to the fields Lucia
in a black hood and shawl
prods a mule. Francesca follows,
drawing her shaded by chestnut vines,
wading through streams of waterflag.
Now, her mornings begin with the sound

of Lucia mowing or sheaving.
Francesca forgets to sketch, begs
Lucia to put the grainsacks down and talk.
Lucia is selling her hair to a man, for wigs.
For two feet of thick black braid
she gets a cotton handkerchief to cover

her head in church. Francesca finishes
the drawings. She doesn't draw the church.
Lucia appears turning water
into wine. A halo surrounds her head.
She knots her scarf in shadow.

THE HISTORY OF SOUND

An occasional flutter
of the hem of a gown;
stuttering, nouns, whole
sentences. Then someone
hung a bell inside a church

and everything changed—
all that emptiness in space—
the spire thrown up there,
humming in the dark,
attracting all kinds of things.

And over the water,
downshifting over boats,
clouds formed *glories*—
upended rainbows town officials
claimed were signs that they,

their scrolls, words,
everything they governed,
would someday be reduced to
marsh-pipe cries. No one
thought of emigrating.

Now the belfries have been
bricked up for centuries.
Each time monks ring the hour,
only cows look up, as if
the air were disturbing itself.

V

SKIPSTONE

1.

Sometimes my lips were flecked
with lipstick or, more often,
the roofing-tar neighbor kids chewed—
my father,
afraid to ground his suspicions
by naming them, bit his tongue.

2.

Turning to a Chagall, you blurt
"I want a divorce...ssh,
we'll talk later." The Louvre darkens
as you push on to the Mondrian room
exclaiming what verve, what
vertiginous color. I look out the window,
where a man is rollerskating,
dressed in a business suit, dignified,
figure-eighting alone through the square.
He keeps glancing over his shoulder,
perhaps worried he might be seen.
Everyone has suspicions. Tonight, taking off
my makeup, hotel mirror glare, why
am I thinking of that old game.
What's its name. Hot summer nights
against our porch steps: white-side-up
meant marry, black-side-up
have a baby, and offsides...of course,
divorce. Skipstone. That's it.

3.

Everything was silent that summer—
even the birdmarket. Misnamed, I was
like those birds that follow tumbleweed miles,
snatching the loosest strands for their nests.
No one understood.
In a bar, a gendarme called himself General;
the bartender kept an albino parakeet
circling colored lights for hours.

4.

A letter from home announces the divorce
is final. I wander the streets, stopping
to give someone directions, to watch a mime
whose specialty is doing famous statues:
Rodin's *Thinker*, a very teetery *Winged
Victory*, and of course the *Venus de Milo*—
I back away, go on. Red light,
traffic jams. The cop waves wearily. I've
had four affairs and my arms ache too.
Somewhere on a deserted boulevard
a new love waits, white face blank, sinking
into the hot asphalt. But if I offer him
recognition, what then, another
perfect parlor, primmed lawn—and
what if he nods in all the right places,
sidestepping vacancies, the slips-into-reverse.
This is habit now, this carrying my house
under my arms without arousing suspicions.

TRESPASSES

France, was it? In the south? I ate rabbit.
Definitely. In Provence.
That day we'd stood before Titian's
"Crown of Thorns." Single figure.
Double versions. In one,
Christ's robe—red
as fresh blood. His robe
in the other—white as snow.
Did serenity overcome
Titian so that in one
he forgot blood or
did he want a resigned subject?

A cold winter. Unusual—for France.
All that snow in the woods.
White covered everything.
The only color:
the brown coat of a deer
lying down for the night.
Like childhood lies down—
the moon cradling
a small circle of color
on top a snowbed,
warming its breath, calling it back.

In Provence, I think. In a pen
behind a four-star
restaurant, rabbits huddled,
their icy feet slipping,
clicking on wire.
Then, to please someone,
I ate what I didn't want to eat.
Nothing will change this.
Survival scars. It's what we do:
feast on what is not ours.

SMALL FACTS

1. Memory

If I lie in the sun on my back
with my eyes open but my mind
far away, on you, do I see the sky?

If a man and a woman concentrate on a hen
to determine the speed of her run
do they see the green hills? Do they
see the largest part of this picture?

Suppose I show you my garden and ask you
later if you saw my roses and you say no
and I say you must have, they are right
beside the summerhouse I showed you,

and what if I take you back there
and there they are: does this mean
only necessary truths are certain?

2. Experience

If I try, I can fit the universe
into a sewing box. I've done it before.
I've stayed up all night embroidering
woods, mending the soft center.

I've knitted pink earthworms that stirred
up so much mud, it filled in
the holes around me. At night
when I teach in a classroom

that feels like a mortuary, unbreathing,
and I scrape *hubris* across the chalkboard
and someone throws up an arm
to interpret a Dickensian passage

at the bottom of the hour, I fold
your letter and fit it into my closed fist.
Believe me, it's nothing
I need to keep. I can throw it

into the ocean and wait for waves
to return a bottle with the letter in it.
If our lives become suddenly beautiful,
is it because all we envy we imitate?

ACADEMIC DREAMLIFE

All day I draw Chinese words,
draw and draw
until they run together,
an inky lake of proverbs.
Beneath their weight
I dream a Chinese poet breaks
into my house, a common
thief, stealing pens, red-lined
pads, my OED, —leaving
in return, six panda bears:
two lounging in the tub,
one sweeping the floor,
three (or four), hard
somehow, to count,
roaming the yard.
Had Gu Cheng done this?
Bei Dao? Lu Lu from Taiyuan?

Two of my bears
(I am beginning to own them)
are reading my European
poetry collection. One, I see,
changing line breaks
in my favorite poem. "You must stop
that," I tell her, a her
at least I think,
such long eyelashes!
Instead, I stop writing.
Jobs done, they
pack, leave me
nothing. Gone, the cupboards,
dishes, all my modern art.

I dust for pawprints,
scrape sinks for fur. I
want to know who
took what. Desperate,
I call the FBI,
offer rewards, search
museums and poetry readings.
One day a forgotten mirror
beckons—all the way
from Taiyuan is Lu Lu—
waving. The bears
are here, he says,
on the Silk Road, renaming
your things:
couch to *birdwing*
rocking chairs to *nightcrawlers*
a Picasso nude to *dandelion*—
I wake to walls so yellow
they glow, to air,
light as scrolls, —as if
some panda bear is turning
poet. But which one?

THERE, WHERE THE GRASS BREAKS

If you see an old lover in the crowd, and he welcomes
your smile and, if later, in the swim of open lips,
lovemaking leads you away from childhood, which fades
like a sienna flower in your naked hand, and something

like faith springs out of your body toward the hands
already printing their stories on your body, don't look
beyond the window to where the grass breaks like a fever
above the entrance to Hell, to where everything breaks:

meadows, mountains, trees. The house, the truth,
the night…This night you are whole—steady pupils,
firm mouth. This is the rhyme scheme of Baudelaire's

footsteps approaching the stranger, Balzac, stopping
in front of him, laughing, as if he'd known him for years,
and Balzac, astonished, as if he'd just met an old friend.

About the Poet

Ginny MacKenzie received her M.F.A. in Creative Writing from Goddard College. Her poems have won numerous literary prizes and have appeared in many magazines and anthologies, including the *Agni Review*, the *Threepenny Review*, *The Nation*, *Ploughshares*, *The Iowa Review*, *Pequod*, *Shenandoah*, the *Mississippi Review*, *Boulevard*, and the *Seneca Review*. Her short stories have appeared in *New Letters*, the *Wisconsin Review*, *Koroné*, the *American Literary Review*, and the *Crab Orchard Review*.. In addition, she is the translator and editor of two contemporary Chinese poetry anthologies, which are part of *New York/Beijing*, a cultural exchange of poets and painters. Recently, her work won the John Guyon Literary Nonfiction Award from Southern Illinois University. She teaches creative writing at the School of Visual Arts and CUNY in New York City.